Thoughts for a Bad Hair Day

Mary Ellen Edmunds

Deseret Book Company
Salt Lake City, Utah

Library of Congress Cataloging-in-Publication Data

Edmunds, Mary Ellen, 1940–

    Thoughts for a bad hair day / Mary Ellen Edmunds.

       p.   cm.

    ISBN 0-87579-952-3

    1. Christian life—Mormon authors. 2. Christian life—Humor.

3. American wit and humor.   I. Title.

BX8656.E37   1995

242—dc20   94-47393

                                               CIP

Printed in the United States of America

10 9   8   7   6   5   4   3   2

To Peggy Park, who can curl *straw!*

Introduction

This book of thoughts can top off or bottom out your bad hair day, help you sort it out, gain perspective, get a grip. Laugh. Cry. Tear out your bad hair.

Some thoughts are meant to help you enjoy your misery, and others are designed to snap you out of it. *Everyone* has bad hair days—those days when nothing seems to go right, and when little tiny things like ugly hair can give you major frustration.

So where do all these thoughts come from? Floating scraps of paper. Old notebooks with many pages unreadable because they've been exposed to The Elements. You. I myself have likely never had an original thought in all my life, but I've heard some good ones. I apologize if I've not given you credit for the great things you've said that are in this book. And I guess, then, that I'm also sorry for the great things you've said that are *not* in this book. Oh shoot. Just can't seem to do it perfectly. Well, anyway, I hope you find something here that will help you through your bad hair days. Enjoy!

God gave us
not only the ability to breathe
but plenty of air.

If at first you don't succeed,
    deny you ever tried.

In my world there are going to be 100 food groups.

Ye shall know the truth, and the truth shall make you mad.

Fun
is probably more
an attitude
than an activity
or an event.

You can pretend you care,
but you can't pretend
to be there.

Be a friend! Loneliness is a terrible disease, but it's not contagious.

Read Golden Books again, curled up in a big chair.

How do I keep from becoming a casual Christian?

In the conversion process there are no coincidences.

If wickedness never was happiness,
then righteousness never was misery.

New friends don't happen that often.

One way to find a lost sheep
is to look where
you think *you'd* go
if *you* were a lost sheep.

Love everyone.
And if you love someone
who doesn't deserve it,
God will certainly
not be mad at you.

They say that if you want to memorize something, you repeat it every hour for a day, every day for a week, every week for a month, every month for a year, and it's yours!

There is so much more to life (or ought to be) than merely surviving.

Mind your own business— find out what it is, and mind it well.

Safe-folded I *rest.*"

(*Hymns*, 1985, no. 108)

One ingredient for which there is no adequate substitute: YOU.

A test of good manners is being able to tolerate bad manners.

Use as directed:
Faith, prayer, priesthood,
kind words.

Love without service,
like faith without works,
is dead.

Make a list of the things you wish *you'd* said.

Oh the joy and wonder of a spiritual sunrise!

When you're having a genuine bad hair day and someone says,
"Have a nice day," simply respond with
"Thanks, but I've made other plans!"

$\mathcal{G}$ood news! Sunsets are free!

If Jesus came to see us and could be with us just a little while,
would He do paperwork?

One can have a whole lot of money
and still be desperately poor.

No contest:
Love is much, much stronger
than hate,
and light will always
dispel darkness.

*I*f you haven't been
through adversity,
where *have* you been?

Carry on! And on! And on!

✣

My mother taught me
that in every home there are burdens and sorrows.

꿈

This just in: It is reported that the following people had just
24 hours every day, divided into 24 equal segments of
60 minutes each: Jesus, Mozart, Gandhi, Joseph Smith,
Michelangelo, Abraham Lincoln, Moses,
and . . . well, you get the idea.

Are there fences in heaven?

Is there an immunization
that will help me shun evil and overcome temptation?

The one with the most fabric wins.
Or the one with the most unfinished projects.

The world has a lot of sinners who think they're saints and saints who know they're sinners.

And then there was the harried mother who said
that one of her acts of charity was to allow her children
to live one more day.

❖

Midge says that forgiving someone seventy times seven
(490 times) doesn't seem terribly difficult
until you're raising teenagers.

❖

Just say NO to ironing!

When you kneel to pray, *wait* until you feel close to Him, until you feel ready to talk to Him honestly and openly.

Look back for the purpose of learning.
Look ahead for the purpose of planning.

No one in the world has written more than Anonymous; she was able to retire early!

Here is Dr. Norm's prescription: Feed a fever. Feed a cold. Feed a headache. Feed allergies. Feed the blues. Feed joy. Feed everything!

Think of all the hair you lose every day.
So probably you've had no two bad hair days
that were exactly alike!

No one likes a frowny face.

I'm a FAN of yours—a Friend And Neighbor.

Wheat and tares grow together,
yes, but the wheat has *got* to remain wheat!

So you're not Betty Crocker . . .
you wouldn't want to wear an apron all the time anyway.

So you want the latest, greatest clothing?
Clothe yourself with Charity.

*T*he only One who could have
thrown a stone . . . didn't.

Somewhere out there
in the universe there's a
huge sign: HELP WANTED.

Think of someone you're mad at. Angry towards.
Begin praying for them. Say their name in your prayers.
Think about them. See what happens.

Have you ever gone a whole day
without breaking the speed limit? WOW!

♡

Separate yourself from worldliness but not
from the world in which all your brothers and sisters live.

Think of ten things you absolutely cannot do without.
Then think of ten things you *can* do without.
(This might be a money-saving tip.)

"Be ye therefore perfect" is a long process, not abracadabra.

Here, courtesy of Goldilocks, is the Three-Bear Theory for
helping others: Not too much, not too little, but *just right.*

*I*f you don't learn
from your mistakes,
what's the use
of making them?

Never read anything
that you wouldn't want to read
out loud—to your mother.

Noah hadn't built an ark before, Nephi hadn't built a ship, and Brigham Young had never crossed the plains.

Surround yourself with sinless people—associate with children as often as you can.

You can't hire someone to go through your sorrow for you.

Carol says, "I sure hope I'm right,
because my mind is made up!"

Many of us don't repent
until we're made to feel uncomfortable.

If we cut out two hours of TV a week, we could make
ten twelve-minute phone calls or write five short notes
or two longer letters.

*I*s anyone out there
using the garage for the car??

*W*hat's the response
of others when they
hear your name?

Pondering is a form of prayer.

Jesus didn't have a closetful of clothes.

Sometimes the *getting ready* is the most fun—for a vacation, for Christmas, for a reunion or whatever.

If you got a hole-in-one every time you went golfing, the enjoyment and challenge of it would soon disappear.

If you begin thinking you're pretty hot stuff, try getting someone else's dog to obey you.

Imagine that you have to have a one-hour promotional video to get into heaven. What would you include? What scenes from your life would you want in that one-hour summary?

Be true to your teeth,
or they'll be false to you.

*I*n the spring of 1820,
a lot of prayers were answered.

Money talks . . . in a foreign language.

Some say, "Money isn't everything, but it's sure a long way ahead of whatever's in second place."

Many of us do receive blessings in disguise—sometimes in such terrible, terrible disguise.

The grass that looks so much greener on the other side
may be artificial turf.

Let's say you're overwhelmed. Way too much to do.
But people just keep asking. Team them up!
Put Needy Person A with Needy Person B
and let them help each other.

Here's a thought from my sister Charlotte: Don't you just *love*
the commandments?? Don't you wish we had *more??*

*A*ppreciate
more than you expect.

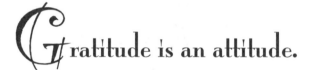

Gratitude is an attitude.

$\mathcal{S}$howing up is 78 percent of life.

There are two ways to win an argument,
and neither of them works or feels good.

Never pass up a chance to be quiet, to just *listen* and *learn*.

The customer is always right but not always pleasant.

Always be at least an inch nicer than is expected.

Three things in life shouldn't be broken:
hearts, promises, and Lladro.

Working allows me
to afford two luxuries I've
grown accustomed to:
eating and living indoors.

*I*t's a miracle
what a smile can do
when someone aims one
directly at you!

Be cheerful and optimistic:
Satisfaction guaranteed.

The year of living righteously.

Which is harder—a choice between good and evil,
or a choice between good and better?

Ignore your teeth and they'll go away.

≋

I have tons of self-discipline and self-control.
Once I went off chocolate for forty-five minutes.
It was one of my finest hours (minus fifteen minutes).

Then there was the time when I exercised one day in a row and
could hardly move, so I knew it was bad for me and I quit.

Wisdom comes from experience, and experience sometimes comes because of a lack of wisdom.

*T*here, there, little
luxury, don't you cry,
You'll be a necessity by and by.

—Quoted by Ezra Taft Benson

$\mathbf{D}$on't make anyone ask for love.

We need to write more love letters.

If you're not going to take time to do it right,
when are you going to make time to do it over?

$\mathcal{S}$ome people are born with rosy red lips.
Mine are off-white.

It could be worse—you could have a hitch in your git-along.

You can never get enough of what you don't need, because
what you don't need never satisfies.

If it's just one person and you,
there's a chance for kindness.

*T*wo wrongs don't make a right, but three lefts do.

14th Article of Faith

We believe in meetings, all that have been scheduled, all that are now scheduled, and we believe that there will yet be scheduled many great and important meetings. We have endured many meetings and hope to be able to endure all meetings. Indeed we may say that if there is a meeting, or anything that resembles a meeting, or anything that we might possibly turn into a meeting, we seek after these things.

When you hear of someone who's done family history work for fifty years and they say they're back to Noah and you're just ready to feel overwhelmed, shout out, "I'm back to my mother!"
You'll feel better.

Don't stop before you've sung the whole song.

A smile is a curve that usually sets things straight.

We spend money
we don't have
to buy things we don't need
to impress people we don't like
. . . who don't come over and
get impressed!

Joy is the flag you fly
when the Prince of Peace is in
residence within your heart.

—Wilfred Peterson

Sign on an office door:
friends welcome; relatives by appointment.

Things to do before the Millennium: Repent and Forgive.

Stop me before I eat something!

$\mathcal{S}$ometimes I seem to be clinging to the law of Moses:
Jab for a jab, hurt for a hurt, silence for silence, push for push,
mean for mean, and so on.

Sandi told me the Eskimos have eighty words for snow.

Peace begins with a smile.

—Mother Teresa

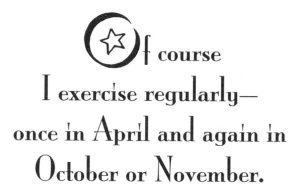

Of course
I exercise regularly—
once in April and again in
October or November.

Honor thy father,
but ask thy mother.

laugh is a smile that keeps on going.

You can even break ice with a smile!

Don said that we are to love God and use things
and that we become miserable if we reach a point
where we use God and love things.

What good is happiness?
You can't get money with it . . .

What do you consider to be the finest, most loving thing you
have done in the past month of your life?

Love is a powerful language.

Fruit is not usually
on the trunk of the tree
or close to it—
it's usually out on a limb.

*T*he words *listen* and *silent*
are both constructed
of the same letters.

Robert E. Lee reportedly gave the following advice to a mother who asked what she could teach her son to help him become a great man: "Teach him to deny himself."

Turn good things into habits.

A while ago I decided to quit stressing about becoming perfect—I'm just trying to be *good*.

HOME is where we came from,
and we're HOMEWARD bound.

❖

If everyone were a star, who would listen and clap?

〰

Beware of "Send no money now!" "No money down!"
"No payments till . . ."

*I*n order to have a second mile, you've got to have a first.

Happiness, like charity, begins at home.

Would it be so bad to die laughing?

Nothing is more beautiful than cheerfulness in an old face.

—Jean Paul Richer

Mirror, Mirror, on the wall, who is fairest of them all?
  If it's me, don't say anything at all . . . "

You cannot hide a change of heart.

Where have all the front porches gone?

It may not taste very good, but pride *can* be swallowed.

Heavenly Father knows best.

You don't have to be poor to be miserable.

A good home
is never an accident.

Another kind of
plastic surgery:
cutting up a credit card.

It's wrong to waste,
no matter how much or how little you have.

In the end, you get what you want.

What goals would you set if you knew you could not fail?

$\mathcal{S}$uccess moves many away from God.

Do unto others as you would have others do unto you . . .
even if they never, never do.

If there is no malice in your heart,
there can't be none in your jokes.

—Will Rogers

People pray for you
whom you don't even know.

*D*ecide what a beautiful day
it's going to be for you
before checking the weather.

When you've got all your merit badges,
there's not much to stick around for.

Richard said the fun of the pun is in the tone of the groan.

If I could just see around the bend.

It's a long road back from mistakes.

Those are my principles—and if you don't like them,
I have others.

Good might make us stop striving for Great.

*M*any live lives
of quiet inspiration.

Grace is
when God helps us
when we don't deserve it.

God has never broken a promise.

WOO: Window Of Opportunity. WOO-WOO: Two windows!

There are no shortcuts to any place worth going.

Joy is not in things. It is in us.

—Benjamin Franklin

I'm not afraid of *heights* so much as *widths* . . .

If everyone in the world would gain ten pounds,
we'd all be closer together.

*D*o unto others
as if *you*
were the others.

$\mathcal{J}$oy
is the serious business
of Heaven.

–C. S. Lewis

One joy scatters a hundred griefs.

—Chinese Proverb

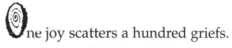

Happiness is a way station between too little and too much.

—Channing Pollock

One thing I know: the only ones among us who will be
really happy are those who will have sought
and found how to serve.

—Albert Schweitzer

Happiness makes up in height what it lacks in length.

—Robert Frost

※

Laughing in the darkness
can many times bring back the light.

A person will be called to account on Judgment Day
for every permissible thing he might have enjoyed but did not.

—Talmud

Get your sails ready,
and by and by
God will send the wind.

*N*ot what we have
but what we enjoy
constitutes our abundance.

Comedy is an escape, not from truth but from despair,
a narrow escape into faith.

—Christopher Fry

Why not learn to truly enjoy the little things—for in life
there are so many of them.

Let's say you make at least two people happy every week during
the coming year—with a kind word, a smile, a note of apprecia-
tion, a bit of time. That comes to at least one hundred people.
Imagine! And what if you were to increase that to making five
people a week happy, or two every other day . . .

Wholesome laughter has been known to dispel anger and soften hearts, to mend fences and erase differences, to enhance unity and quiet rage.

If I can't find joy here and now, will I find it anywhere?

Visitors are always appreciated—sometimes when we arrive, and sometimes when we leave.

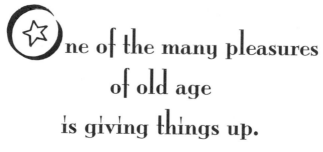

One of the many pleasures
of old age
is giving things up.

—Malcolm Muggeridge

*I*f you deviate an inch
in direction,
you'll lose a thousand miles
in destination.

The smile you give to someone else today
might not make a difference for them. But then again . . .

What would, for you, be an ideal Sabbath day?
Plan one. Live one.

Prepare in leisure to use in haste.

Pure gold fears no fire.

꠸

If you get bored, try a new hobby,
like maybe collecting rare barbed wire or counting sand.

♡

Three things are very difficult:
to keep a secret, to forget having been hurt,
and to make good use of leisure.

Enjoy life!
This is not a dress rehearsal.

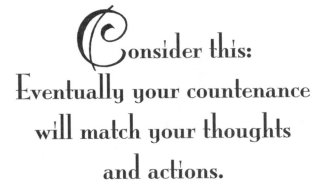

Consider this:
Eventually your countenance
will match your thoughts
and actions.

We have freedom of choice, yes,
but not freedom *from* choice.

If I worry a lot about tomorrow today it won't help
with tomorrow's challenges,
but it sure might mess up today's joy.

It's not a bad thing to be very happy
if you're willing to share it generously.

Decide to get a big kick out of little things more often!

Most folks are about as happy
as they make up their minds to be.

—Abraham Lincoln

You can't cut down seeds to build houses.

*T*ell someone
you plan to love them
for a long, long time.

A good sense of humor
helps me handle
who I am right now
on my way to becoming
who I'd really like to be.

Mercy and forgiveness are quiet things.

It's a longer road back if you've burned your bridges.

One-seventh of your life is spent on Mondays—
but one-seventh is spent on Fridays, too.

Mary decided to stay home with her little son Dayne
because, she said, "He's learning too much too fast
for me to trust someone else to teach him."

Have you ever been so frightened
that you felt like a million-year-old tree:
petrified?

It's hard to be a shadow leader
if you don't know where the sun is.

*D*on't just view flowers
from a galloping horse
or a speeding train.

Cleanliness is next to impossible—
you put down something, and it grows! Try putting a piece of
paper down somewhere and watch it happen.
Soon it'll be a stack.

There's more energy in a pound of desire
than in a pound of talent.

Laughter is an instant vacation.

—Milton Berle

They say a clean desk
is the sign of a troubled mind.

※

Maybe it's better to wear out than rust out—keep going!

※

The hills are full of marble before the world is full of statues.

Where much is expected,
much is given
in the way of help.

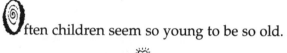ften children seem so young to be so old.

There doesn't seem to be much relationship
between *things* and *happiness*.

Humor is tragedy plus time.

—Mark Twain

Nothing is quite so frustrating as to argue with people who know what they're talking about.

Have you heard? Boomerangs are coming back!

When you share a smile with someone, you have discovered the universal language.

$\mathcal{S}$ometimes
there's less danger
in the things we fear
than in the things we desire.

Laughter
is something so contagious,
like a yawn, that perhaps we
could start an epidemic!

Much of the most effective communication
requires no words at all.

≈

Even the gods love jokes.

—Plato

※

Even if you can't find anything to laugh about,
laugh on credit.

113

Life is full of routine miracles.

Some of my best Christmas gifts
were purchased at the "five and dime."

There are three rules for getting organized,
but, unfortunately, no one can remember what they are.

My way of joking
is to tell the truth.
It's the funniest joke
in the world.

—George Bernard Shaw

Heavenly Father doesn't use phone mail. Every conversation with Him is live.

The art of medicine consists of amusing the patient while nature cures the disease.

—Voltaire

There are many shades of gray, yes, but there is still white.

—Harvey Cox

Tears and laughter are so closely tied together that it's sometimes hard to separate them.

As I learn to laugh at myself
I gain a wonderful new perspective about life
and the sometimes almost overwhelming situations
in which I find myself.

It seems that in my happiest times I'm not sick very often.

In all comedy there is something regressive that takes us
back to the world of play we first knew as children.

—Roger Polhemus

Our Heavenly Father
knows the rest of the story.

*T*hey are rich
who know
when they have enough.

Why does it seem easier to feel
that others have shared in our failures
than it is to remember those who have shared
in our achievements?

He has the right to criticize who has the heart to help.

—Abraham Lincoln

You cannot move within and stand still without.

Happiness is having a large, loving, caring, close-knit family—in another city.

—George Burns

Anyone who's been convinced by logic can be unconvinced by logic . . . and often is.

Cory says, "When it stops hurting, it'll feel better."

*I*t was a dark and stormy night . . . but I chose to enjoy it!